Starters

Logger's Dining Table, Hartwick Pines State Park

Cherry Blossoms

Deviled Eggs

6	hard-cooked eggs
1/2	teaspoon salt
1/4	teaspoon pepper
1/2	teaspoon dry mustard
3	tablespoons mayonnaise
1/2	teaspoon red wine vinegar
	Paprika

Place eggs in a saucepan and cover with cold water to at least one-inch above eggs. Heat to boiling. Reduce to simmer and cook 15 to 20 minutes. Immediately crack shells and plunge eggs into cold water to prevent further cooking and darkening of the yolks. Peel eggs. Cut each in half lengthwise. Remove yolks; mash with a fork. Add seasonings. Spoon yolk mixture into egg whites, heaping up slightly. Dust lightly with paprika.

CUCUMBER-ASPARAGUS BOATS

Michigan is 3rd in the nation for asparagus production.

4	ounces cream cheese, at room temperature
1	tablespoon lemon juice
6	spears cooked asparagus, chopped
1/4	teaspoon mild curry powder
1	tablespoon poppy seeds
2	medium cucumbers, peeled, quartered & seeded

Combine cream cheese, lemon juice, asparagus, and curry powder in a small bowl. Mix well. Spoon into cavity of prepared cucumbers. Sprinkle with poppy seeds. Chill. Slice into 1-inch pieces. Insert a toothpick in the center of each piece to serve. Makes about 30 pieces.

TOMATO and BASIL BRUSCHETTA

Very ripe tomatoes may be used by mashing them almost to a puree and smearing on top of bread.

2	cloves garlic, roasted and mashed
4	Roma tomatoes
2	large yellow tomatoes
1/4	cup fresh basil leaves, chopped into thin strips
	Salt and freshly ground black pepper
6	slices of Focaccia or other country-style bread
3	tablespoons virgin olive oil
1	clove cut fresh garlic
	Sprinkle of fresh grated Parmesan cheese

Place individual unpeeled garlic cloves on a baking sheet, sprinkle with salt and drizzle with oil. Bake about 30 minutes at 375 degrees until tender. Place tomatoes under broiler (or on grill) just long enough to blister skins. When cooled, cut each tomato in half, remove seeds and dice. Combine mashed garlic, diced tomatoes, and half of the basil in a medium bowl. Season with salt, pepper, and drizzle with olive oil. Set aside at room temperature for 15 minutes or more.

Rub bread with the cut surface of the fresh garlic clove. Brush with a little olive oil. Place on the grill or under the broiler until slightly toasted. Turn over and toast the other side. Immediately, remove toast and top with tomato mixture. Sprinkle the remaining basil and Parmesan cheese over top. Makes 6 large slices or 12 halves.

LAKE MICHIGAN BLINI

These delicious treats use local Whitefish caviar. Blini are a kind of white-or-wheat flour yeast pancake that is very popular in Russia.

1	recipe buckwheat pancakes (see "Breads")
2	cups sour cream
1/2	cup caviar

Thin buckwheat batter with 1/4-cup warm water to make silver-dollar-size pancakes. Mix half of sour cream with caviar and spread on half the hotcakes. Cover each with another pancake. Place a dollop of plain sour cream on top of each. Serve as canapes. If you prefer, make 5-inch pancakes, spread with caviar cream mixture and roll cakes up to serve as a first course. Place a scoop of plain sour cream on each roll.

SMOKED WHITEFISH COCKTAIL APPETIZER

Whitefishes are related to the salmon family and are similar in appearance to trout, but have smaller mouths and larger scales.

2	pounds smoked whitefish
1	cup mayonnaise
1	tablespoon dry mustard
1	tablespoon chives, minced
1	large tomato, peeled, seeded and diced
1	tablespoon dry sherry
	Freshly ground black pepper.

Several hours ahead, bone and flake fish and refrigerate. Mix mayonnaise with mustard, chives, and diced tomato. Fold in flaked chilled fish, then stir in sherry. Add ground pepper to taste. Serve on toast rounds. Yields 12 servings.

Frankenmuth

Solera Mushroom Soup

From St. Julian Wine Company, Michigan, who developed this soup featuring their award-winning Solera Cream Sherry.

3	tablespoons butter		1	teaspoon fresh thyme, minced
1	teaspoon oil		1/4	teaspoon each: fresh parsley, minced, garlic powder and ground black pepper
1	pound mushrooms, chopped			
3	tablespoons onion, chopped		1/2	teaspoon mustard powder
1	tablespoon flour		1/2	cup skim milk
1/2	cup cream sherry		1/2	cup half and half
3-1/4	cups beef broth		2	teaspoon carrots, shredded (optional)

Heat butter and oil over medium heat in a large saucepan. Add mushrooms and onions and sautè for 7 minutes. Sprinkle flour over mixture and stir. Blend in the cream sherry and cook for 1 minute. Transfer this mixture to a blender and puree. Pour beef broth into blender. Add all seasonings. Blend until thoroughly mixed. Return puree to saucepan. Stir in milk and cream. Heat until warmed through but do not boil. Serve with a sprinkling of shredded carrots as garnish, if desired. Serves 6.

ROOT VEGETABLE SOUP

2	tablespoons butter
2	leeks, thinly sliced
2	cups new potatoes, peeled and diced
4	cups carrots, peeled and diced
4	cups turnips, peeled and diced
6	cups chicken stock
1/2	teaspoon dried thyme
	Salt and freshly ground pepper

In a large stockpot, melt butter. Add leeks and cook, covered, over low heat for 10 minutes or until softened. Do not let them brown. Add remaining vegetables and stock and bring to a boil. Reduce heat and simmer, covered, for 1 hour.

Puree soup in a blender a little at a time. If too thick, add more stock. Return to saucepan to reheat. Add seasonings.

OPTIONAL CREAMED VERSION:

3	tablespoons butter, unsalted
1	cup whipping cream
	Julienne of carrots for garnish

Add cream while soup is reheating. Just before serving, whisk in butter. Garnish with carrot shavings.

BLACK BEAN SOUP

Michigan's dried black beans are exported all over the world.

1	pound black beans
1	onion, chopped
1	carrot, chopped
1	stalk celery, sliced
6	cloves garlic, peeled
1	bouquet garni (parsley, thyme, tarragon, bay leaf, celery leaves)
3/4	pound smoked ham hock
10-12	cups chicken stock
1	tablespoon chili powder
1	tablespoon ground cumin
1	fresh Serrano chili, minced
	Salt to taste
1/2	cup sour cream
2	tablespoons milk
	Salsa to garnish

Rinse and sort beans. Place in stock pot. Add enough cold water to cover beans and soak overnight. Drain and return to stockpot with onion, carrot, celery, garlic, bouquet garni, ham hock, and enough chicken stock to cover. Bring to a boil, skimming as necessary. Reduce heat and simmer, partially covered, about 2 hours. Add more chicken stock if necessary to keep ingredients submerged. Stir to prevent sticking.

Remove from heat and stir in chili powder, cumin, and chopped fresh chili. Puree bean mixture in food processor or blender until smooth. Return soup to a clean saucepan, adding enough cooking liquid to obtain a soup-like consistency. Reheat and season to taste with salt. When ready to serve, whisk sour cream and milk together. Ladle hot soup into warmed soup bowls. Drizzle sour cream over each serving and top with salsa. Serves 6 to 8.

FRESH SALSA

2	cups ripe tomatoes
1/4	cup red onion, finely chopped
1	Serrano chili, minced
1/4	cup cilantro, chopped
1/2	teaspoon salt
2	tablespoons fresh lime juice
2	teaspoons extra-virgin olive oil

Place chopped tomatoes in a bowl. Add remaining ingredients, except olive oil. Stir well to combine. Let rest one hour at room temperature or overnight in the refrigerator. Before serving, bring to room temperature. Drain off any accumulated water and stir in olive oil.

Holland at Tulip Time

Cream of Tomato Soup

3-1/2	cups chopped, seeded tomatoes		WHITE SAUCE	
3	sprigs parsley, minced		3	tablespoons butter
6	whole cloves		3	tablespoons flour
1	bay leaf		1	teaspoon salt
3/4	teaspoon whole black pepper		1/4	teaspoon pepper
3	slices onions		2	cups milk
1	teaspoon sugar			
1	teaspoon salt			
2	cups white sauce			

In a saucepan, combine all ingredients except white sauce. Simmer about 5 minutes until tomatoes are mushy. Rub tomato mixture through a sieve or process in a blender or food processor. Add boiling water, if necessary to reach 2 cups puree.

To make white sauce: Melt butter over low heat; add flour, salt, and pepper. Stir until well blended. Remove from heat. Gradually stir in milk and return to heat. Cook, stirring constantly, until thick and smooth. Add tomato puree and serve warm. Serves 4.

SWISS CHARD with RAISINS and PINE NUTS

Other greens such as kale or spinach can be used instead of Swiss Chard.

3	tablespoons seedless dark raisins
1/4	cup hot water
1	pound Swiss chard, trimmed and cut into 1-inch-wide strips
1	tablespoon olive oil
2	garlic cloves, finely chopped
1/2	teaspoon salt
2	tablespoons pine nuts

Combine raisins and water in a small bowl. Set aside. In a large pot of boiling water, blanch the chard for 6 minutes; drain well. In a large skillet, heat the oil over low heat. Add the garlic and cook 2 minutes. Add the chard, tossing to coat with oil. Stir in the raisins with their soaking liquid. Add salt and cook 3 minutes longer, or until the pan juices have thickened slightly. Stir in the pine nuts and cook 1 minute longer. Serves 4.

ACORN SQUASH with PECANS

2	acorn squash, about 1/2 pound each
	Salt and white pepper
1/3	cup unsalted butter
1-1/2	cups pecan halves

Cut each squash in half and remove seeds and fiber. Sprinkle cavities liberally with salt and pepper. Melt butter in saucepan; add pecans and toss to coat. Scoop equal portions of pecans into squash. Place squash halves into a shallow baking dish. Add 1 inch of water to bottom of dish. Bake at 375 degrees until squash is tender, about 40 minutes. Occasionally stir nuts to keep them moistened with butter while baking. Serves 4.

BROILED TOMATOES with HERB TOPPING

3	large ripe tomatoes
4	tablespoons mayonnaise
4	tablespoons Parmesan cheese
2	tablespoons green onion, minced
1	clove garlic, minced
1	tablespoon fresh basil, chopped

Cut tomatoes in half horizontally and let come to room temperature. Mix topping ingredients together. Divide among tomato halves and spread evenly. Broil 5 inches from heat until browned. Serves 6.

MICHIGAN BAKED BEANS

In pioneer Michigan, cooks baked beans in a dripping pan with salt pork covering the top. Beans were cut out of the pan in slices and served with homemade tomato catsup.

2	pounds dried navy beans
9	cups water
1	pound salt pork, diced
3	tart apples, peeled, cored and coarsely cut
1	medium onion, chopped
3/4	cup brown sugar, firmly packed
3	teaspoons dried mustard
3	tablespoons vinegar
1/4	teaspoon pepper

Wash beans and soak overnight in water. Drain. Place beans in stockpot with salt pork. Cook until beans are tender, about 1 hour. Pour bean mixture into a bean pot or heavy casserole dish. Add remaining ingredients and bake, covered, 6 hours at 300 degrees. Add more water during cooking if necessary. Yields 10 servings.

CLASSIC RATATOUILLE

A specialty from Provence with obvious overtones of Italian and Spanish cuisine.

1	medium-size eggplant, peeled, sliced and salted
3	cups onions, chopped
1/2	cup light olive oil
3	medium-size ripe tomatoes, peeled, seeded and chopped
3	medium-size zucchini, peeled and sliced
3	red peppers, halved, seeded and cut into strips
1	clove garlic, crushed
1	bouquet garni (celery, leek, bay leaf, thyme & parsley) Salt and freshly ground pepper

Salt the eggplant slices and set aside for about 20 minutes. Cook onions in olive oil in a large covered pan over low heat for 10 minutes or until softened. Add tomatoes and cook 3 minutes. Dry eggplant slices with a paper towel and chop coarsely. Add eggplant, zucchini, peppers, garlic, and seasonings. Stir. Cover and simmer over low heat for 1 hour or until vegetables have released their liquid and are softened and blended. To reduce liquid, uncover and continue cooking over low heat another 20 to 30 minutes. Serves 4 to 6.

THREE-BEAN SALAD

2	tablespoons red wine vinegar
1	tablespoon fresh parsley, chopped
1	teaspoon each: fresh oregano and basil chopped Salt and pepper to taste
1/2	cup olive oil
1/2	cup canned red kidney beans
1/2	cup canned white kidney beans
1/2	cup canned garbanzo beans
1/2	cup canned golden hominy
1	tomato, finely chopped
1	red onion, finely chopped
1/2	cup finely chopped celery

Combine vinegar, herbs, salt, and pepper into medium-size salad bowl. Slowly drizzle in olive oil and stir with a fork. Rinse beans in a colander under cold water to remove any canned taste. Rinse hominy in a fine strainer. Drain thoroughly and stir into salad bowl. Toss to coat with vinaigrette. Finely dice tomato, onion, and celery and toss into bean mixture. Let stand at room temperature for 1 hour or refrigerate overnight. Serves 4.

FETTUCCINE and ASPARAGUS with CREAMY MOREL SAUCE

The asparagus harvest is commemorated at the National Asparagus Festival every second week of June in Oceana County.

3/4	ounce dried morel mushrooms
4	teaspoons minced shallot
3	tablespoons cold unsalted butter
1/2	cup dry white wine
1	cup chicken stock Salt and pepper to taste
1	cup heavy cream
1/2	pound thin asparagus, trimmed and cut into 1-inch pieces
3/4	pound fresh fettuccine or 8 ounces dry

Add hot water to cover morels and soak for thirty minutes or until they are softened. Drain, wash well, and halve any large ones lengthwise. In a saucepan, saute the shallot in 1 tablespoon of the butter over medium heat until softened. Add wine and bring to a boil. Add the stock, the morels and salt and pepper to taste; bring to a boil, then simmer until liquid is reduced to about 3/4 cup. Add the cream, bring to a boil, then simmer the sauce, stirring occasionally, for 8 to 10 minutes, or until it is thick enough to coat the spoon.

In a saucepan of boiling salted water, cook asparagus for 2 to 3 minutes, or until it is just tender. Drain and rinse under cool water. Cook fettuccine in boiling salted water 3 minutes for fresh or 8 minutes for dried. Drain well and transfer to a bowl. While pasta is cooking, reheat sauce until hot, stirring in the additional 2 tablespoons butter. Toss the pasta with the sauce and the asparagus. Serves 4.

Detroit

Swiss Asparagus Au Gratin

When sun and water conditions are right, the amazing asparagus stalk will grow as much as one inch an hour! The stalks are snapped by hand or machine at seven and one half inches.

1/2	cup water
1-1/2	pounds asparagus spears, trimmed
1/2	cup Swiss cheese, finely shredded
1/2	cup dry bread crumbs
2	tablespoons butter or margarine
1/2	teaspoon dry mustard
1/8	teaspoon pepper

Bring 1/2 cup water to boil in 10-inch skillet; add asparagus. Cook 2 minutes; drain. (Asparagus will still be crisp.) Place in a 10x6-inch-baking dish. Mix remaining ingredients; sprinkle over asparagus. Bake 15 minutes at 350 degrees or until cheese mixture is lightly browned. Makes 4 servings.

PARMESAN PASTA FLORENTINE

1/2	cup milk
1/2	cup chicken broth
1	10-ounce package chopped spinach, thawed and drained
1/2	cup chopped onion
2	cloves garlic, minced
2	tablespoons butter
1/3	cup Parmesan cheese, grated
1/4	teaspoon pepper
8	ounces linguine, cooked and drained

Place milk, broth, and spinach in blender or food processor container fitted with steel blade; cover. Blend until smooth. Sautè onion and garlic until tender. Add spinach mixture. Cook over low heat 5 minutes, stirring occasionally. Add cheese and pepper, stirring 1 minute or until slightly thickened. Pour over linguine; mix lightly. Serves 4.

CREAMED ASPARAGUS

To serve to the table family style, chop asparagus spears into 1-inch lengths and stir together with cream sauce.

1	pound fresh or frozen asparagus, cooked
1/2	cup water
4	tablespoons butter
4	tablespoons flour
1/2	teaspoon salt
1/4	teaspoon pepper
2	cups milk
1	slice buttered toast per serving

Optional seasonings include capers, grated cheese, diced cucumbers, chopped hard-cooked eggs, mustard, chopped mushrooms, lemon juice, paprika, or other favorites.

Boil asparagus in a saucepan in enough water to cover until tender, approximately 10 minutes for fresh or 7 minutes for frozen. Drain and set aside.

Melt butter over low heat, add flour, salt, and pepper; stir until well blended. Remove from heat. Gradually stir in milk; return to heat. Add optional seasoning if desired. Cook and stir until sauce is smooth and thick. Place asparagus spears on toast. Serve sauce over top.

MOREL MUSHROOMS in WINE SAUCE

From L. Mawby Vineyards, Michigan, who suggest that this dish be accompanied by their "Eric the Red" wine.

4	cups fresh morel mushrooms
2	tablespoons water
2	tablespoons olive oil
1	medium onion, halved and slivered
3	cloves garlic, minced
2	cups chicken broth
2	tablespoons soy sauce
1/2	cup dry red wine
2	tablespoons balsamic vinegar
1/2	teaspoon thyme
1/4	teaspoon sage
1	teaspoon salt
2	tablespoons cornstarch

Wash mushrooms in cool water. Soak in salted water 20 minutes. Drain. Rinse several times to remove all traces of dirt from the honeycombed caps. Drain well and dry with paper towels. Cut in half or into 2-inch pieces. Put in a pan with about 2 tablespoons water. Cover and steam over low heat for 20 minutes. Drain. Reserve mushroom liquid.

Sautè onions and garlic in olive oil over medium heat, stirring frequently until caramelized. Mix all remaining ingredients, except cornstarch, together in a bowl. Add to onion/garlic mixture. Stir in mushroom water. Cover and simmer 10 minutes. Remove one-half liquid from pan. Return morels to pan. Add cornstarch to the one-half liquid and whisk. Stir into pan and simmer a few minutes until starch thickens and becomes clear. Serve immediately over linguine pasta or rice. Serves 4.

Meats

Amish wheat harvest, Mid-Michigan

Copper Miner, Houghton-Hancock

Corned Beef & Beet Hash

1-1/2	cups cooked corned beef
2	potatoes, cooked and diced
1-1/2	cups beets, cooked, drained & chopped
1	medium onion, chopped
1/3	cup milk or cream
	Salt and freshly ground pepper to taste
1/4	cup bacon drippings or other oil for frying

Combine all ingredients except cooking oil. Heat a heavy 10-inch skillet and add oil. When oil is heated, spread corned beef mixture evenly over pan; press down to form a smooth cake. Cook slowly about 40 minutes over low heat until browned. Turn out onto a plate, invert onto another plate and slide back into skillet to brown other side. Serves 4.

MICHIGAN-STYLE PASTIES

These all-in-one lunches were favorites of Cornish miners who settled in Michigan in the 1800's and are still family favorites today.

1	pound beef top round steak or sirloin tip, cut into 1/2-inch cubes
2	potatoes, diced, or 3 potatoes, if not using turnips
2	medium turnips, diced (optional)
1	medium onion, minced
4	tablespoons butter
2	teaspoons salt
1/4	teaspoon pepper

In a large bowl, combine meat, vegetables, and seasonings.

GRANDMA LOU'S NEVER-FAIL PASTRY

2-1/4	cups flour
1/2	teaspoon salt
1/2	teaspoon baking powder
1	cup shortening

Mix in another bowl:

1	egg yolk
2	teaspoons vinegar
	Enough water with above to make a cup

In a medium bowl, combine flour, salt, and baking powder. With a pastry blender, or two knives, cut shortening into mixture to resemble coarse crumbs. Sprinkle water/egg yolk mixture into flour mixture one tablespoon at a time, mixing lightly with a fork after each addition until dough begins to hold together. Shape dough into a ball. Divide into 4 pieces. On a lightly floured board, roll each pastry ball into a circle about 9 inches in diameter and 1/8 inch thick. Trim edges. Place pastry circle on a large cookie sheet. Spoon 1/4 of meat/vegetable mixture onto one half of the circle and spread to make an oval mound. Put in 1-tablespoon butter cut into small bits. Gently pull pastry edges up around meat mixture; pinch firmly to seal. Pasty should be the shape of a half moon. Trim edges to 1/2 inch and fold over and crimp. Repeat to make 4 pasties. (Optional: Re-roll trimmings to strips about 10 inches by 3 inches. Cut lengthwise into 12 thin strips. Fold 3 strips into a braid. Moisten sealed edge with milk; place braid on edge, pressing lightly along the entire edge. Repeat with remaining strips.) Bake in 400-degree oven about 1 hour until golden. Makes 4 pasties.

MELT-IN-YOUR-MOUTH PETITE FILLET of BEEF

Venison steaks are equally good prepared this way. For especially tender venison, cut steaks 2 inches thick and pound seasonings and butter into meat with a wooden mallet.

4	8-ounce Filet Mignon steaks, 1-1/2 to 2 inches thick
6	tablespoons butter, softened
	Salt and freshly ground pepper
	Parsley for garnish

Preheat broiler to highest temperature with rack set to hold filets 5 to 6 inches from the heat. Dry filets with a paper towel. Rub 1/2 tablespoon butter per steak over the top and bottom. Season with salt and pepper. Place filets on a broiler rack and broil 4 to 6 minutes per side for rare or 6 to 8 minutes per side for medium. Place ovenproof serving plates on the bottom rack of the oven to heat during cooking. When the meat is done, remove hot plates, and place a tablespoon of butter on each. Place steak over butter as it sizzles and melts. Place a pinch of parsley on top of meat. Serve the dishes to the table sizzling hot. Serves 4.

GROUND VENISON MEATLOAF

Serve as a main course or in small slices, chilled, as an appetizer.

1	tablespoon vegetable oil
1	onion, finely chopped
1-1/2	pounds ground venison
3/4	pound ground pork
1	egg
1/2	cup soft fresh bread crumbs
1/2	cup milk

1	teaspoon salt
1/2	teaspoon ground allspice
1/2	teaspoon rubbed sage
1/4	teaspoon pepper
1	cup crabapple jelly, melted (for sauce, optional)
1/2	cup port wine (for sauce, optional)

Heat oil in large skillet; sautè onion until softened. Transfer to a large bowl. Add venison, pork, and all remaining ingredients. Mix well to combine. Place mixture into a greased 9x5x3-inch loaf pan and smooth top with spatula. Cover with aluminum foil. Bake at 350 degrees for 1 hour. Cool 10 minutes in pan; drain and invert loaf onto serving platter. For sauce, melt crabapple jelly and combine with wine. Serve warm sauce over the loaf. Serves 6.

GERMAN PICKLED BEEF ROAST

This is one of the most famous food contributions from our German settlers.

1	4-5 pound beef pot roast, with bone
1-1/2	cup water
1/2	cup dry red wine
1	stalk celery with leaves, chopped
8	black peppercorns
4	whole allspice
4	whole cloves
2	bay leaves

Place beef in a deep glass or stainless steel bowl. Combine the marinade ingredients in a medium saucepan and bring to a boil. Boil 2 minutes and let cool. When cooled, pour marinade over the meat, turning roast to coat all sides. Cover and refrigerate 2 or 3 days, turning the meat several times each day. Several hours before serving, drain marinade and reserve. Pat meat dry with a paper towel.

To cook:

3	tablespoons oil
1	onion, chopped
1	stalk celery, chopped
1	carrot, chopped

1/2	cup water
1/2	cup red wine
8	gingersnaps, rolled thin or 2 tablespoons flour

Heat oil in a large Dutch oven. Add the meat and brown on all sides, turning frequently, about 30 minutes. Remove the meat. Pour off all but 2 tablespoons fat. Sautè the onion, celery, and carrot until tender, about 10 minutes. Return meat to the pan. Strain the reserved marinade and discard vegetable pulp. Add 1/2 cup water to strained marinade and pour it around meat. Reduce heat to low and simmer, covered, about 3 hours until roast is tender. Remove the meat to a platter and keep warm. Remove the marrow from the bone and stir it into the pan sauce. Puree the pan sauce in a blender and return it to the pan. Add red wine. Bring to a simmer and add gingersnap crumbs (or flour). Simmer and stir until sauce is thickened. Serve meat sliced with thickened sauce. Serves 6.

RACK of LAMB with MINT SAUCE

Michigan mint growers produce over 50,000 pounds of spearmint each year.

| 2 | 4-rib racks of lamb, 1-1/4 to 1-1/2 pounds each |
| | Salt and freshly ground pepper to taste |

MINT SAUCE

1/2	cup mild vinegar
1/4	cup water
1/4	cup sugar
1/2	cup chopped mint leaves, no stems
1-1/2	tablespoons chutney, optional

Season the lamb with salt and pepper. Place each rack, fat side up, in a shallow roasting pan. Cover the bone ends with aluminum foil to prevent burning before the lamb is done. Roast in a preheated 350-degree oven for about 35 minutes per pound or until meat thermometer registers about 175 degrees according to desired doneness. Slice chops and serve with Mint Sauce or Mint Jelly. Serves 2. For Sauce: Combine all ingredients and let stand 1 hour or more. Add more sugar if desired.

Sunflowers, Montcalm County

Ground Beef Eggplant Main Dish

2	medium-size eggplants, about 2 pounds
1	pound ground beef
2	tablespoon vegetable oil
1	large can (1 pound) stewed tomatoes
1	8-ounce can tomato sauce
1	teaspoon salt
1	teaspoon leaf oregano, crumbled
1/4	teaspoon garlic salt
1/2	cup grated Parmesan cheese

Trim ends from eggplants; cut a thin slice lengthwise from each; scoop out centers, being careful not to break shells. Place shells in a shallow baking pan. Chop scooped-out centers. Brown ground beef in skillet, stirring to crumble. Add chopped eggplant. Stir and cook 10 minutes. Stir in tomatoes, tomato sauce, salt, oregano and garlic salt. Simmer, stirring several times, 25 minutes. Stir in cheese. Spoon into eggplant shells. Bake in oven at 350 degrees 25 minutes or until shells are tender. To serve, cut each in half. Serves 4.

BIGOS (HUNTER'S STEW)

1	pound pork, cubed
1/4	pound bacon cut in 2-inch pieces
1/4	pound garlic sausage, sliced
3	onions, chopped
1	head cabbage, shredded
1/4	pound mushrooms, sliced
1	small can tomato puree
2	cloves garlic, crushed
1	teaspoon cumin seed
2	teaspoons paprika
1	bay leaf
	Salt to taste
2	cups white wine

Dice bacon and pork; brown well in a large Dutch oven along with the sausage and onions. Add cabbage, mushrooms, tomato puree, garlic and seasonings. Stir until well combined. Add wine. Cover and cook in oven at 350 degrees for 1-1/2 hours or until done. Serve hot with dark bread. Serves 6.

VEAL LOIN CHOPS with QUICK BROWN SAUCE

4	veal loin chops, (bone in)
	flour, salt & pepper
	Butter or margarine
1	pound spinach, cleaned and stemmed

Dredge chops in flour and season to taste with salt and pepper. Sautè in butter until golden brown on both sides. Place in baking dish and bake at 475 degrees 20 to 25 minutes or until done as desired. Remove from dish and keep warm. Spoon 1 to 2 tablespoons veal drippings into sauté pan and add spinach. Cook, stirring, until spinach is barely wilted. Place spinach on serving platter and top with chops. Brush chops with quick brown sauce. Makes 4 servings.

QUICK BROWN SAUCE

1/4	cup butter or margarine
1/4	cup flour
2	beef bouillon cubes
2-1/2	cups boiling water
2	sprigs parsley
1/2	small bay leaf
	Dash thyme
1/2	cup Sherry

For sauce: Melt butter in saucepan. Blend in flour and cook, stirring, about 5 minutes until mixture is medium brown in color. Dissolve bouillon cubes in boiling water. Gradually stir into flour mixture until smooth. Stir in parsley, bay leaf, and thyme. Cook over low heat about 15 minutes, until thickened, stirring occasionally. Strain. Add Sherry and keep warm in double boiler. Makes about 2 cups.

BEEF POT ROAST

This best-ever pot roast is worth the effort of starting a day ahead.

4-5	pounds lean boneless chuck roast or 7-bone roast
1	quart water
1	tablespoon sugar
1	stalk celery, sliced
2	onions, sliced
1	tablespoon salt
1	teaspoon pepper
1/2	teaspoon each: allspice, cinnamon and curry powder
1	teaspoon dry mustard
1-1/2	carrots per person
2	medium potatoes per person

Combine water, sugar, celery, onions, salt, pepper, and spices. Pour mixture over meat and allow to stand overnight in refrigerator. Remove the meat and cook in a 300-degree oven for 3 to 4 hours. During the last hour, add the carrots and potatoes, placing carrots on top of meat. Thicken the drippings, if desired, to make gravy to serve with the roast and vegetables. Serves 6 to 8.

Poultry & Game Birds

Farm Scene near Lansing

Peach orchard at blossomtime

Chicken with Parsley Dumplings

1	stewing chicken, 4 to 5 pounds, cut up	1	carrot, pared and sliced
4	cups water	1	teaspoon salt
1	large onion, sliced	1/4	teaspoon pepper
1	cup celery and leaves, chopped	1/2	cup cold water
		1/3	cup flour

Place chicken in Dutch Oven with the 4 cups water, onion, celery and leaves, carrot, salt and pepper. Heat to boiling. Cover tightly and reduce to simmer. Simmer 1-1/2 to 2 hours, or until chicken is tender. Remove chicken from broth; cool and slip off skin. Strain and measure broth. Add water, if needed, to make 5 cups. Press vegetables through strainer into broth. Return broth to Dutch Oven. Heat to boiling. Combine 1/2-cup water with 1/3-cup flour. Stir to make a smooth paste. Whisk into hot broth. Cook, stirring constantly, until thickened. Season with salt and pepper to taste, if needed. Return de-boned chicken to broth in Dutch Oven. Heat slowly to boiling while stirring up parsley dumplings (directions, next page).

PARSLEY DUMPLINGS

1-1/3	cups all-purpose flour
2	teaspoon baking powder
1/2	teaspoon salt
3	tablespoons vegetable shortening
1/3	cup parsley, chopped
3/4	cup milk

Sift flour, baking powder, and salt into a medium-size bowl. Cut in shortening with a pastry blender until crumbly. Stir in milk, just until moist. Drop dough by spoonfuls on top of steaming chicken. Reduce heat to low. Cover and steam for 30 minutes. Do not peek or dumplings will not become puffy and light. Arrange chicken and dumplings on a serving platter and pass gravy separately. Makes 6 servings.

GOOP

Although the name is unappetizing, Goop is a popular covered dish to take to supper socials.

2	tablespoons butter
1	3 to 4 pound chicken, cut into serving pieces
1/2	pound veal
1	teaspoon salt
	Freshly ground pepper
	Water to cover
1	8-ounce package noodles
1-1/2	cups Cheddar cheese, grated
2	tablespoon butter (separate from above)
1	medium onion, chopped
1	green pepper, chopped
1/2	pound mushrooms, sliced
1	cup pitted black olives

Melt butter in a Dutch Oven over medium heat. Add chicken and brown on all sides. Add veal. Sprinkle salt and pepper over all. Add enough water to cover meat. Cover and simmer for 2 hours. When veal is fork tender, remove chicken and veal to cutting board. Skin and bone chicken and cut veal into bite-sized pieces.

Cook noodles according to package directions. When noodles are cooked, drain and add grated cheese. In a skillet, melt 2 tablespoons butter and saute onion, green peppers, mushrooms, and olives. When vegetables are tender, spread over noodles and top with chicken and veal. Serves 6 to 8.

ROASTED WILD CANADIAN GOOSE with FRIED APPLES

This is a dish so rare and wonderful that for centuries, it has been served before kings and queens.

1	Canada goose, 5 to 6 pounds
	Coarse salt and freshly ground pepper
5	tart apples
1	stalk celery, sliced in 2-inch sections
1/4	cup butter
3	tablespoons brown sugar
3	tablespoons dried currants, soaked in a little red wine (Bordeaux or Burgundy)
1/4	cup apple brandy

Preheat oven to 400 degrees. Rinse cavity of goose, dry with paper towels and rub in coarse salt and fresh pepper. Stuff with 1 apple, quartered, and the celery pieces. Thoroughly prick skin all over with a large fork. Place on a rack in a deep roasting pan. Pricking the goose will eliminate any need for basting, as fat will bubble up through the holes and trickle down over the body to baste itself. Place goose breast-side-down in hot oven for 15 minutes. Reduce oven to 325 degrees and roast about 2-1/2 hours or until the drumstick meat is soft. A great deal of fat will be produced during cooking. After an hour and a half, pour off all drippings and reserve. Return goose to oven. About 20 minutes before serving, prepare fried apples by coring and peeling remaining apples. Slice in thick pieces. Heat butter in skillet and fry apple slices in foaming butter, turning and adding the brown sugar after 5 minutes. Continue to fry until golden, then add currants. Place apples around goose on a warm platter. Just before serving, pour flaming apple brandy over all. Makes 4 servings.

Round Island Lighthouse and Grand Hotel, Mackinac Island

Roasted Wild Duck with Wild Rice

2	wild ducks, dressed
1	recipe Marinade for Game
	Salt and freshly ground pepper
1/4	cup butter
1	apple, quartered
1	carrot, sliced
1	onion, quartered
3	cups chicken broth
2	green onions, chopped
1	cup wild rice
1/2	cup golden raisins
1/3	cup brandy
	Watercress and orange slices

MARINADE FOR GAME

3/4	cup port
1-1/4	cups olive oil
3	sprigs tarragon
2	stalks parsley
1	celery stalk, chopped
1	onion, diced
6	peppercorns
1/8	teaspoon sage
1	teaspoon lemon peel

Combine and mix marinade ingredients. Put ducks in a plastic bag and pour marinade over them. Refrigerate for 12 hours, turning occasionally. Drain ducks and pat dry. Sprinkle inside and out with salt and pepper. Brown on all sides in butter in a large skillet. Place half the apple, onion and carrot in each duck cavity. Put the ducks in a casserole to fit snugly and add 1 cup of the chicken broth. Cover and roast at 350 degrees for 1-1/2 hours or until ducks are tender. Remove ducks from casserole; discard the apple, onion, and carrot. Place ducks on a serving platter and keep warm while making rice.

For rice, skim excess fat from the casserole drippings. Add enough chicken broth to make 2-1/2 cups liquid. Pour it into a heavy pot; add the green onions and bring to a boil. Wash the rice and drain; then stir into the broth. Add raisins and brandy and bring to a boil again, stirring frequently. Reduce heat and simmer 40 minutes or until rice is tender, adding chicken stock if needed. Place the rice on the platter with the ducks. Garnish with watercress and orange slices. VARIATION: If you precook the wild rice, you may stuff the ducks with it in lieu of the vegetables. Makes 4 servings.

Fish & Shellfish

South Haven Harbor

Upper Tahquamenon Falls

Stewed Fish With Beans

Any combination of fish may be used, including perch, pike, blue gill, whitefish, lake herring, bass, catfish, crappie, carp, or chubs.

2	pounds white fish fillets, cut into 1-inch chunks		1	onion, thinly sliced
1/2	pound large shrimp, peeled and deveined		1/2	cup almonds, toasted and finely chopped
	Salt		1/2	teaspoon black pepper
4	tablespoons olive oil		1	fresh chili pepper, chopped
4	garlic cloves, minced		3	tablespoons fresh Italian parsley, chopped
2	ripe tomatoes, peeled, seeded and sliced		2	cups cooked white beans
1	green sweet pepper, seeded, deribbed and sliced crosswise			

Sprinkle fish and shrimp lightly with salt and hold in the refrigerator until ready to use. Heat olive oil in a large Dutch oven; saute garlic, tomatoes, and sweet pepper until pepper is tender, about 10 minutes. Use a slotted spoon to remove vegetables to a bowl. Add onions to the oil and saute until golden, about 10 minutes. Return the tomato-pepper mixture to the pan and add the almonds, black pepper, chili pepper, and parsley. Stir well and add water to cover the vegetables by about 1/2 inch. Bring to a boil. Add the fish and reduce heat to simmer. Cover and simmer for about 10 minutes, then add the shrimp and cook for 2 minutes longer. Stir in the cooked white beans and heat through. Taste and adjust seasoning as desired. Serves 6.

OVEN-BAKED FISH & CHIPS
(with Whitefish, Carp or Bass Fillets)

Any thick white fillets may be prepared this way.

4	tablespoons butter
2	tablespoons oil
2	pounds red or white potatoes, sliced 1/4-inch thick
2	pounds thick whitefish fillets (or similar fish)
	Salt and freshly ground pepper to taste

Preheat oven to 425 degrees. Put 2 tablespoons butter and 2 tablespoons oil in a shallow-sided baking pan large enough to hold potatoes laid in a single shallow layer. Place the pan in the oven to melt the butter. Peel potatoes and slice them thin with a food processor blade or mandoline. When butter is melted, remove pan from oven, stir potatoes into hot butter and oil; sprinkle with salt and pepper. Return to oven and bake 10 minutes. Remove pan and turn potatoes with a spatula. Return and bake 10 minutes more. Check again and bake another 10 to 20 minutes or as necessary to brown, turning often. When potatoes are browned, place the whitefish fillets on top of them, dotting the fish with the remaining 2 tablespoons butter. Bake for 8 to 12 minutes, depending on thickness. Fish is done when it is opaque when tested with a thin-bladed knife. Serves 4.

SMOKED SALMON with NOODLES and DILL SAUCE

2	tablespoons minced shallot
3/4	cup dry white wine
1-1/4	cups heavy cream
3/4	pound fresh egg noodles or 8 ounces dried
3	tablespoons snipped fresh dill
1/2	pound smoked salmon, thinly sliced, cut along the grain into 2x1/2-inch strips
	Salt and pepper to taste

Combine shallot and wine in a saucepan; bring to boil, then simmer until wine is reduced to 2 tablespoons. Stir in the cream, bring to a boil, then reduce heat, and simmer 5 minutes. Keep sauce warm. Prepare pasta in a kettle of boiling salted water, cooking 3 minutes for fresh or 6 minutes for dried noodles, or until it is al dente. Rinse the pasta under cold water, drain well, and transfer it to a large bowl. Bring the sauce to a boil, then immediately remove it from heat and stir in the dill. Pour the sauce over the noodles and toss. Stir salmon in gently and season with salt and pepper. Serves 4.

SALMON PIE

1	15-ounce can salmon
1/2	cup milk or as much as needed to make 1 cup when mixed with salmon liquid
2	eggs, slightly beaten
1/2	teaspoon salt
1	tablespoon grated onion
1	tablespoon minced parsley
1	tablespoon lemon juice
2	cups mashed potatoes
1/2	cup Cheddar cheese, grated

Preheat oven to 375 degrees. Grease a 10-inch round deep-dish pie plate. Drain salmon; reserving liquid. Add enough milk to liquid to make 1 cup. Flake salmon. Add liquid and other ingredients, except potatoes and cheese. Mix lightly. Turn into pie plate. Spread mashed potatoes over the top evenly and score with a knife blade. Sprinkle grated cheese over top. Bake 25 minutes. Cut in wedges. Serves 6.

LAKE MICHIGAN WHITEFISH STEAMED over COURT BOUILLON with SAUCE

COURT BOUILLON

3	quarts water
1	tablespoon butter
2	teaspoons salt
	Juice of 1 lemon
2	peppercorns
1	bay leaf
1/4	cup diced onion

Combine ingredients and bring to a boil. Simmer for 20 minutes. Use to steam fish.

1 whole whitefish, 2 to 3 pounds

Place fish on an oiled rack above pan with 2-inches Court Bouillon. Use a fish steamer or a piece of cheesecloth to protect fish from breaking. Cover and simmer 15 to 20 minutes. Test doneness by pricking with a fork. Fish is done when flesh is white and opaque throughout and translucence is nearly gone. (Fish will continue to cook after being removed from steamer). Set aside and keep warm. Strain Court Bouillon to make sauce.

SAUCE

2 cups strained Court Bouillon
1 cup milk
2 tablespoons flour
4 tablespoons milk
  Salt and pepper to taste
  Chopped hard-boiled egg, optional

In a saucepan, add milk to Court Bouillon and bring to a boil. Reduce heat. Blend flour into 4 tablespoons milk and add to hot bouillon. Stir over low heat until sauce thickens. Add seasonings to taste. Serve over fish.

A WEALTH OF SMELT

These silvery scaleless fish, 3 to 4 inches long, run in the spring and fall in tributaries of the Great Lakes. Seasonal smelt runs are a time of traditional celebration in Michigan when the fish are so numerous that they can be scooped up in bushel baskets.

SIMPLE SAUTÈED SMELTS

5 - 6 smelt per person, gutted with heads removed
  Salt, pepper, lemon juice, flour, butter or olive oil

Cut 3 diagonal gashes on each side of fish. Sprinkle with salt, pepper, and lemon juice. Cover and let stand 10 minutes. Roll in flour. Saute in butter or olive oil a few minutes until cooked through and golden brown on both sides, about 5 to 6 minutes.

OVEN-BAKED SMELT SCALLOP

2 pounds smelt, cleaned and cut into serving size pieces
1-1/2 cups coarsely crushed crackers
2 cups milk
2 tablespoons butter
1-1/2 tablespoon minced onion
1/2 teaspoon salt
1/4 teaspoon pepper
1/2 cup dried breadcrumbs, buttered
  Dash of paprika

Arrange fish and crackers in layers in a greased casserole. Combine milk, butter, onion, and seasonings; heat to boiling point. Pour over fish and crackers. Melt an additional tablespoon butter to stir into 1/2-cup fine breadcrumbs. Top casserole with buttered crumbs and a dash of paprika. Bake in a hot oven at 425 degrees for 15 to 20 minutes or until browned. Make 4 to 6 servings.

BATTER FRIED SMELT

May use any pan-sized fish including blue gill, crappie, chub, lake herring, perch, pike or other whitefish.

2 pounds smelt, cleaned and split (5 to 6 per person)
2 eggs
2 tablespoons milk
1/2 teaspoon salt
1/4 teaspoon pepper
1 cup dried bread crumbs, finely ground
1-1/2 cups shortening for deep frying
  Lemon wedges and parsley

Wash fish and pat them dry. Combine the egg, milk, and salt in a bowl and beat until blended. Dip the fish into the egg mixture, then coat well with the crumbs. Melt shortening in large skillet and heat to 375 degrees. Fry the fish until golden brown on both sides. Drain on paper towels. Garnish with lemon wedges and parsley and serve with your favorite fish sauce. Serves 4.

Mackinac Bridge

Grilled Coho Salmon With Cucumber Sauce

1/4	cup mayonnaise		Salt and pepper to taste
1	whole salmon, 4 to 5 pounds, cleaned with head removed	1	onion, sliced
		1	lemon, sliced

CUCUMBER SAUCE

1	cucumber, peeled, seeded and diced	1	tablespoon fresh dill, chopped or
1	stalk celery, finely diced	1	teaspoon dried dill
1	tablespoon lemon juice	1	tablespoon fresh parsley, chopped
1/4	teaspoon salt	3/4	cup plain yogurt
1	teaspoon sugar	1/4	cup mayonnaise
1/4	teaspoon dried tarragon, crumbled		

Pat diced cucumbers and celery with paper towels to remove moisture. Combine with all remaining ingredients. Stir to mix well, then cover and refrigerate up to 2 days. Bring to room temperature before serving. Makes 2 cups. Fish preparation, next page.

Prepare grill. Spread half of mayonnaise on a large piece of heavy-duty aluminum foil. Place salmon over mayonnaise. Season cavity with salt and pepper and tuck in the onion slices and half the lemon slices. Spread remaining mayonnaise over top of salmon and cover with remaining lemon slices. Close foil and fold edges to make a sealed pouch. Place on grill rack at 375 to 400 degrees and cook 8 to 10 minutes per inch of thickness, or bake in a preheated oven at 400 degrees. Test fish with a fork and when it flakes, it is ready to serve. Serve immediately with cucumber sauce. Serves 8 to 10.

SALMON LOAF

1	pound salmon, cooked or canned (2 cups)
3/4 - 1	cup milk
1-1/2	cup soft bread crumbs
2	tablespoons chopped sweet pickle
2	teaspoon lemon juice
1/2	teaspoon salt
1/4	teaspoon pepper
1	egg, slightly beaten

If using canned salmon, drain and reserve liquid. To liquid, add enough milk to measure 1 cup. Flake salmon with a fork. Combine all ingredients. Press into a greased small loaf pan. Bake in a moderate oven at 375 degrees for 25 to 30 minutes or until browned. Serve with Mock Hollandaise Sauce.

MOCK HOLLANDAISE SAUCE

Make Medium White Sauce as follows:

4	tablespoons butter
4	tablespoons flour
1	teaspoon salt
1/4	teaspoon pepper
2	cups milk

Melt butter over low heat; add flour, salt, and pepper. Stir until well blended. Gradually stir in milk and cook slowly, stirring constantly, until sauce is thick and smooth. To make Mock Hollandaise, add the following ingredients:

3	tablespoons lemon juice
6	tablespoons butter
	Dash of cayenne
3	egg yolks

Just before serving medium white sauce, add lemon juice and butter 1 tablespoon at a time, and cayenne. Heat thoroughly and gradually stir a little of the hot sauce over 3 slightly beaten egg yolks. Stir egg yolk mixture into remaining sauce and cook over very low heat for 2 to 3 minutes, stirring constantly. Makes 2-1/2 cups. Serve with vegetables or fish.

PAN-FRIED PERCH with TARTAR SAUCE

Other commercially raised fish, which may be used in this recipe, include catfish and three varieties of trout.

2	pounds perch, gutted and split or filleted
2 - 4	tablespoons oil
2	tablespoons butter
1	cup cornmeal or flour
1	teaspoon salt
1/4	teaspoon pepper

Wash fish well; wipe dry with a paper towel. Heat butter and oil 1-inch deep in a large non-stick skillet until hot but not smoking. Mix salt and pepper with cornmeal or flour. Dredge fish in cornmeal/flour until well covered. Place in hot oil in skillet and raise heat to high. Cook on both sides until nicely browned and fish flakes when tested, about 8 to 10 minutes depending upon thickness. Serve with tartar sauce. Serves 4.

TARTAR SAUCE

1	cup mayonnaise
2	tablespoon chopped onion
2	tablespoons chopped parsley
2	tablespoons chopped capers
1	tablespoon chopped pickles
1	tablespoon chopped olives
	Dash of prepared horseradish to taste

Mix well. Serve with fish. Makes 1-1/2 cups.

Breads

BUCKWHEAT PANCAKES

This is a favorite dish for breakfast with molasses or for blini rolled with various fillings for appetizers. Blini pancakes have been made in Russia from time immemorial.

1	package active dry yeast
2	cups warm water
1	cup buckwheat flour
1	cup unbleached flour
1	teaspoon salt
1/4	teaspoon baking soda
1	tablespoon butter, melted
2	tablespoons molasses for breakfast cakes

The night before, dissolve the yeast in the warm water and stir in both flours and salt. Cover and set in a warm place. When ready to use, dissolve the baking soda in the melted butter and add to the flour mixture. Add molasses, if desired. For blini, omit molasses and add about 1/4-cup warm water to thin batter to the consistency of heavy cream. Test cakes on a butter-greased griddle heated to 400 degrees. If batter is too thin, stir in a small amount of buckwheat flour; if too thick, add a little more water. Pour 2 tablespoons or more of batter onto griddle, depending on size desired. Do not let sides touch. Turn when bubbles appear on the surface and bake until lightly browned on the other side. For stuffed pancakes, use a 6-inch crepe pan and fill completely with a thin layer. Makes about 2 dozen small cakes or 1 dozen large cakes.

GOLDEN CAKE-LIKE CORNBREAD

1-1/4	cups all-purpose flour
3/4	cup cornmeal
2	tablespoons baking powder
1/3	cup sugar
3/4	teaspoon salt
1-1/4	cups milk
1/4	cup shortening
1	egg

Preheat oven to 400 degrees. Combine flour, cornmeal, baking powder, sugar, and salt in a medium bowl. Add the milk, shortening, and egg. Mix only until ingredients are well combined. Place batter in a greased 8x8-inch pan. Bake for 25 to 30 minutes until the top is golden brown. Let the cornbread cool slightly before slicing. Yeilds 9 pieces.

HONEY BUTTER

1/2	cup butter, softened
1/3	cup honey

To make honey butter: Mix on high speed to whip butter and honey together until light and fluffy.

ZUCCHINI BREAD

Grated carrots or apples can be substituted for zucchini in this basic quick bread.

3	cups flour
1	tablespoon baking powder
1	cup sugar
1/2	teaspoon salt
2	eggs, slightly beaten
1/3	cup butter, melted
1-1/4	cups milk
1	cup grated, drained zucchini, carrots or peeled apple
1/2	cup chopped pecans or walnuts, optional

Combine all dry ingredients. Beat egg with butter and milk. Make a well in the center of the dry ingredients and pour milk mixture into it, along with the zucchini, carrots, or apple. Using a large spatula, combine ingredients quickly, folding together rather than stirring. Batter will be lumpy. As soon as ingredients become moistened, put batter into a greased 9x5-inch loaf pan. Bake about 1 hour at 350 degrees, or until a toothpick inserted into center of loaf comes up dry. Cool 10 minutes on a rack before removing from pan. Makes 1 loaf.

BLUEBERRY MUFFINS

Michigan leads the nation in blueberry production, producing one-third of all blueberries eaten in the United States.

1	egg
1/4	cup salad oil
1	cup milk
2	cups flour
1/2	cup sugar
3	teaspoons baking powder
1/2	teaspoon salt
1	teaspoon ground cinnamon
1	cup fresh blueberries or 3/4 cup frozen blueberries (thawed and drained)

Preheat oven to 400 degrees. Grease bottoms of 12 muffin cups. Beat egg and combine with oil and milk. Add dry ingredients, mixing just until moistened. Batter will be lumpy. Fold in blueberries. Fill muffin cups 2/3 full. Bake 20 to 25 minutes or until golden brown. Remove from oven and let rest 5 minutes before removing muffins from pan. Yields 12 muffins.

PINE NUT PUMPKIN BREAD

1	cup brown sugar
1/2	cup granulated sugar
1	cup fresh cooked or canned pumpkin
1/2	cup salad oil
2	eggs, unbeaten
2	cups flour
1	teaspoon baking soda
1/2	teaspoon salt
1/2	teaspoon cinnamon
1/2	teaspoon nutmeg
1/4	teaspoon ginger
1	cup raisins
1/2	cup pine nuts
1/4	cup water

Combine sugars, pumpkin, oil, and eggs. Beat until well blended. Sift together flour, soda, salt, and spices; add to pumpkin mixture and mix well. Stir in raisins, nuts and water. Spoon into greased and floured 9-inch loaf pan. Bake at 350 degrees for 1 hour.

Cherry Pie

No area in the world produces more red tart cherries than Michigan. Every year in early July, people flock from around the country to beautiful Traverse City, the "Cherry Capital of the World" to celebrate this favorite fruit.

Pastry for a two-crust pie

1	cup sugar (add another 1/4 cup if using fresh cherries	2	16-ounce cans tart cherries or 1-1/2 pounds fresh tart cherries
3	tablespoons cornstarch	1/2	teaspoon almond extract
1/4	teaspoon salt	4	drops red food coloring, if desired
		2	tablespoons unsalted butter, cut into small bits

In a medium saucepan, combine sugar, cornstarch, and salt. Drain and measure the liquid from the canned cherries. Add about 1-1/4 cups of drained liquid to saucepan. Set cherries aside. Stir the cherry liquid into the sugar mixture until no lumps remain; heat to boiling, stirring frequently. Continue cooking until mixture is thickened and slightly translucent. Remove from heat, stir in the reserved tart cherries, almond extract and if desired, food coloring.

Roll out bottom pastry between 2 sheets of lightly floured waxed paper to make a circle about 1/8-inch thick and 1 inch larger in diameter than the top of the pie pan. Fold over rolling pin and place into a 9-inch pie pan, unfold, and fit loosely. Trim edges even with outside of the rim. Spoon in the cherry filling, mounding it higher in the center. Dot with butter. Roll out top pastry and place over filling. Seal edges and flute or crimp to make a standing edge to help prevent pie filling from bubbling over. Cut several slits in top crust to vent pie. Sprinkle the remaining 1-teaspoon sugar over top crust. Bake on lower shelf of hot oven at 400 degrees for 35 to 40 minutes. Yields 6 - 8 servings.

BLACK WALNUT CAKE with PENUCHE FROSTING

1/2	cup butter or margarine, at room temperature
1/2	cup brown sugar
1/2	cup granulated sugar
1	teaspoon vanilla extract
2	eggs
1	cup chopped black walnuts
2	cups cake flour
1	tablespoon baking powder
1/2	teaspoon salt
3/4	cup milk

Prepare two 8-inch round cake pans by greasing sides and bottom. Put a circle of waxed paper in bottom of each pan. Preheat oven to 375 degrees. Cream butter, sugars, and vanilla together. Add eggs, one at a time and beat well to mix. Stir in chopped walnuts. Premix cake flour, baking powder, and salt. Add flour mixture alternately with milk, stirring just enough to blend. Divide batter into cake pans. Bake about 25 minutes or until a tester inserted in center comes out clean. Cool on wire rack.

FROSTING

1	cup brown sugar
1/2	cup granulated sugar
	Dash of salt
1/3	cup milk
2	tablespoons butter
1	tablespoon corn syrup
1/2	teaspoon vanilla
	Whole black walnut halves for top decoration

For frosting, mix sugars, salt, milk, butter, and corn syrup in a small saucepan and bring slowly to a boil, stirring constantly. Boil 1 minute. Cool to lukewarm and add vanilla. Beat until thick and creamy. Spread frosting between layers and on top and sides of cake. Decorate top with walnut halves. Serves 8.

RHUBARB PIE

For a popular variation, substitute fresh sliced strawberries for half the rhubarb and use a lesser amount of sugar.

	Pastry for a 2-crust pie
1-1/2	cups sugar
1/3	cup flour
1/2	teaspoon grated orange peel
4	cups fresh tender pink rhubarb, cut into 1/2-inch pieces
2	tablespoons butter
1	tablespoon sugar

Combine sugar, flour, and orange peel. Arrange half of rhubarb into pastry-lined pan; sprinkle with half the sugar mixture. Add remaining rhubarb and sugar mixture. Dot with butter. Cover with top crust. Cut several slits to vent pie. Seal and flute edges. Sprinkle top crust with sugar. Cover edge with a 2 to 3-inch strip of aluminum foil to prevent excessive browning. Remove foil after 30 minutes. Bake about 45 minutes at 425 degrees. Serves 6 to 8.

BURGUNDY BERRY PIE

	Pastry for a two-crust pie
1	cup sugar
3	tablespoons cornstarch
	Dash salt
2	cups frozen blueberries (without sugar)
1-1/2	cup whole cranberries

Combine sugar, cornstarch, and salt. Mix berries together. Stir sugar mixture into berries. Spread into pastry-lined 9-inch pie pan. Cover with top pastry; flute edges and cut vents in crust. Bake at 425 degrees until pastry is lightly browned and juices bubble through vents. Serves 6 to 8.

COOKED GRAPE JELLY

5	pounds grapes approximately to yield 4 cups juice
1	cup water
1/4	cup lemon juice
1	package fruit pectin or 3 ounces liquid fruit pectin
5-1/3	cups sugar
1/4	teaspoon margarine or butter

Wash and crush grapes into a saucepan. Add 1-cup water and lemon juice. Bring to a boil. Reduce heat and simmer, covered, for 10 to 15 minutes, or until pulp is softened. (Add a little water if necessary to keep grapes from sticking to the pan). Extract juice through a sieve or several layers of damp cheesecloth stretched across a bowl large enough to hold the strained juice. Let stand overnight in the refrigerator. Sediment will settle on bottom of container. Slowly pour juice from container, being careful not to disturb sediment.

Measure juice into a large saucepan. Add pectin, mixing thoroughly. Bring to full, rolling boil, stirring constantly to prevent scorching. Reduce heat to medium and stir in sugar, mixing well. Bring to full boil, stirring constantly, and boil for 2 minutes. Margarine or butter can be added to minimize foaming. Remove from heat. Skim off foam. Fill sterilized jars quickly to 1/8-inch from tops. Wipe off rims. Cover quickly with sterilized flat lids. Screw bands tightly. Invert jars 5 minutes, then turn upright. After 1 hour, check seals. Store in a cool, dark location for up to 12 months. Yields 7 eight-ounce jars.

NO-COOK STRAWBERRY FREEZER JELLY

3	cups juice extracted from about 3 quarts strawberries
1/4	cup lemon juice
1	package fruit pectin or 3 ounces liquid fruit pectin
1	cup light corn syrup
4-1/2	cups sugar

Wash, stem, hull and grind or crush berries to a pulp. Pour through 3 layers of cheesecloth to extract juice. Let drip into bowl until dripping stops. Measure carefully and add up to 1/2-cup water for exact measure. Add lemon juice. Gradually stir in pectin; mix thoroughly. Set aside for 30 minutes, stirring every 5 minutes to dissolve pectin completely. Pour corn syrup into juice mixture; mix well. (This prevents sugar crystallization during freezer storage.) Stir in sugar gradually. Continue stirring to dissolve completely. Pour into sterilized plastic containers to within 1/2-inch of tops. Wipe edges of containers. Cover with sterilized lids. Freeze for up to 12 months. Yields 7 eight-ounce jars of jelly.

APPLESAUCE

2	pounds cooking apples, cored and quartered
1-1/2	cups water
1/2	cup sugar or to taste
	Spices to taste (cinnamon, nutmeg, mace, or fresh mint)
	Grated lemon or orange rind, optional

Wash, core, and quarter apples. Put in saucepan with water. Cover and cook over low heat until soft. Strain through a food mill or sieve. Add sugar, more or less as desired. Return to heat and boil just long enough to dissolve sugar. Lemon juice or grated lemon or orange rind may be added, if desired.